Things Up Close

by Alice Boynton

Red Chair Press   Egremont, Massachusetts

Look! Books are produced and published by Red Chair Press:

Red Chair Press LLC   PO Box 333   South Egremont, MA 01258-0333

www.redchairpress.com

FREE Educator Guides at www.redchairpress.com/free-resources

Publisher's Cataloging-In-Publication Data

Names: Boynton, Alice Benjamin.

Title: Things up close / by Alice Boynton.

Description: Egremont, Massachusetts : Red Chair Press, [2019] | Series: Look! books. Look closely | Interest age level: 004-007. | Includes Now You Know fact-boxes, a glossary, and resources for additional reading. | Includes index. | Summary: "In Things Up Close, young readers view common objects-a pencil, sponge, toothbrush, and seashell-from a new perspective and learn uncommon facts about each one."--Provided by publisher.

Identifiers: ISBN 9781634406697 (library hardcover) | ISBN 9781634406734 (paperback) | ISBN 9781634406772 (ebook)

Subjects: LCSH: Implements, utensils, etc.--Juvenile literature. | Nature-Miscellanea--Juvenile literature. | Athletics--Equipment and supplies--Juvenile literature. | CYAC: Implements, utensils, etc. | Nature. | Athletics--Equipment and supplies.

Classification: LCC TX298 .B69 2019 (print) | LCC TX298 (ebook) | DDC 643.6 [E]--dc23

LCCN: 2018955660

Photo credits: cover, pp. 1, 7, 10–11, 16, 21 (bottom), 22 (middle) iStock; pp. 4, 6, 8, 10, 12, 14, 15, 18, 20, 21 (top), 22 (top, bottom) 24 Shutterstock.

Printed in United States of America

0519 1P CGF19

Table of Contents

4

Very Handy

You use it every day.
The longer you use it,
the shorter it gets.
What is it?

It's a pencil. It's made of wood. But what's in the center? It's **graphite** or lead (*led*). That's the part you write with. It can write 45,000 words. Wow, that's a lot of words to know.

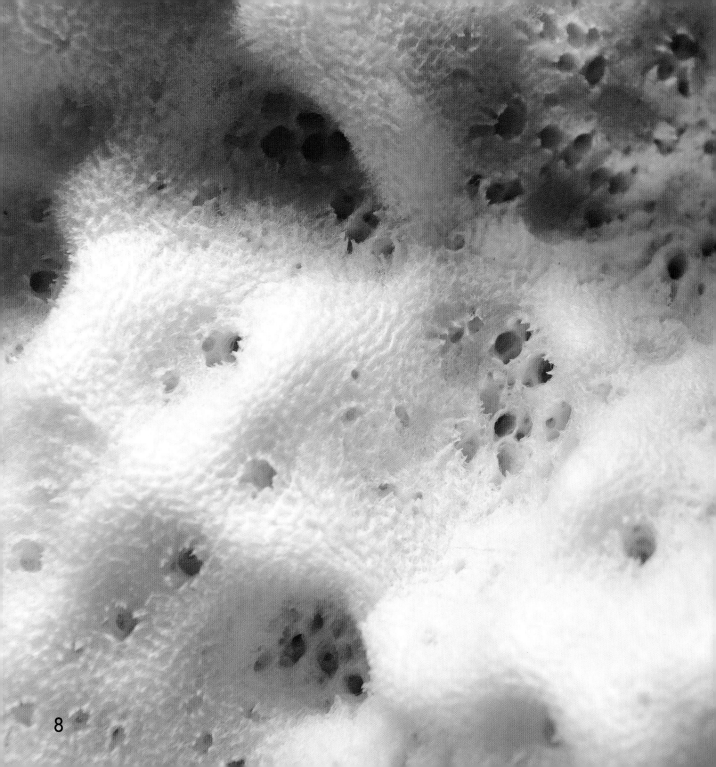
8

Squeeze Me!

It has many, many holes. But it can still hold lots of water. What is it?

It's a sponge (*spuhnj*). Sponges live in the **ocean**. People once thought they were plants. But no! They're animals! They can live for a long time. Some are 200 years old.

GOOD to KNOW

Spill something? Grab a sponge! Most kitchen sponges are machine-made.

1, 2, 3, Smile!

It has a head.
But it doesn't
have eyes.
You put paste on it.
But it's not sticky.
What is it?

It's a toothbrush.
It keeps teeth clean.
Germs in your mouth
grow on your teeth.
Germs cause **cavities**.
Oh, no! So brush
every day—after
breakfast and before
bed. Good job!

Anybody Home?

You find it
on the beach.
It comes from
the water.
It can be
big or small,
plain or fancy.
What is it?

It's a seashell. An animal once lived inside. Maybe it was a snail. The shell was the animal's **skeleton**. The hard shell **protected** its soft body. When the animal died, its shell was left.

GOOD to KNOW

Hermit crabs move into empty shells. As the crab grows, it moves to a bigger shell.

Test Yourself!

What are these things?
There are no clues
for you, but you have
seen them all.
Look closely!

1 sneakers

2 basketball

3 soapsuds

Words to Keep

cavities: holes in teeth

graphite: a material found in rocks under the ground and used in pencils

ocean: the large body of salt water that covers much of planet Earth

protected: kept something safe

skeleton: the hard shell on the outside of some ocean animals, like snails and crabs

Learn More at the Library

Books (Check out these books to learn more.)

Carle, Eric. *A House for Hermit Crab.* Aladdin Paperbacks. 2014.

Jones, George. *My First Book of How Things Are Made* (Cartwheel Learning Bookshelf). Scholastic. 1995.

Web sites (Ask an adult to show you these web sites.)

Amazing Crabs Shell Exchange | Life Story | BBC
https://www.youtube.com/watch?v=f1dnocPQXDQ

How It's Made: Pencils
https://www.youtube.com/watch?v=vlptoTkE25Q

How It's Made: Toothbrushes
https://www.youtube.com/watch?v=deOqWyRp-XI

The wonderful world of sea sponges - BBC Wildlife
https://www.youtube.com/watch?v=BW05vMziy2o

Index

About the Author

Alice Boynton has over 20 years of experience in the classroom. She has written many books on how to teach with nonfiction. She looks closely at all the things around her at home in New York City.

24